THOMAS EDISON

World-Changing Inventor

by Katherine Krieg

Content Consultant
Paul Israel
General Editor, Thomas Edison Papers
Rutgers University

Core Library

An Imprint of Abdo Publishing
www.abdopublishing.com

www.abdopublishing.com

Published by Abdo Publishing, a division of ABDO, PO Box 398166, Minneapolis, Minnesota 55439. Copyright © 2015 by Abdo Consulting Group, Inc. International copyrights reserved in all countries. No part of this book may be reproduced in any form without written permission from the publisher. Core Library™ is a trademark and logo of Abdo Publishing.

Printed in the United States of America, North Mankato, Minnesota
042014
092014

Cover Photo: SuperStock/Glow Images
Interior Photos: SuperStock/Glow Images, 1; Anonymous, 4; AP Images, 6, 12, 37, 39; Con Tanasiuk/Design Pics/Corbis, 8; Library of Congress, 11, 26, 34; Brady-Handy Collection/Library of Congress, 17, 43; Red Line Editorial, 18; Bettmann/Corbis, 20, 25; KJ Bevan/Shutterstock Images, 22; Schenectady Museum/Hall of Electrical History Foundation/Corbis, 28, 45; J. T. Vintage/The Bridgeman Art Library, 32

Editor: Jenna Gleisner
Series Designer: Becky Daum

Library of Congress Control Number: 2014932578

Cataloging-in-Publication Data
Krieg, Katherine.
 Thomas Edison: world-changing inventor / Katherine Krieg.
   p. cm. -- (Great minds of science)
Includes bibliographical references and index.
ISBN 978-1-62403-378-0
1. Edison, Thomas A., (Thomas Alva), 1847-1931--Juvenile literature.
2. Inventors--United States--Biography--Juvenile literature. 3. Electrical engineers--United States--Biography--Juvenile literature. 4. Businessmen--United States--Biography--Juvenile literature.   I. Title.
621.3092--dc23
[B]
                                                            2014932578

CONTENTS

CHAPTER ONE

AN INDEPENDENT INVENTOR

Thomas Edison is one of the most famous inventors in US history. He was granted more than 1,093 patents during his lifetime. These patents meant no one else could make the same products and sell them. We use many of these products every day, such as the lightbulb and the motion picture video camera. Edison inspired others through his work and his dedication to discovery.

Thomas Edison was eager to read, learn, and discover at an early age.

Thomas Edison was born in this house on the banks of the Huron River in Milan, Ohio.

A Curious Child

Thomas Alva Edison was born on February 11, 1847. He was the youngest of seven children. His family called him Al. They lived in Milan, Ohio. Al was curious from a young age. He was always asking questions. He wanted to know how things worked.

When Al was seven years old, his family moved to Port Huron, Michigan. Al went to public school for a little while. Then his mother taught him at home. Al loved to read, and eventually he started reading about science. He found the subject very interesting.

The Grand Trunk Railroad ran through Port Huron. Al liked watching the trains. He spent time learning about how they worked. When he was 12 years old, he got a job at the train station. He sold candy, books, and newspapers to people on the trains. He sometimes read the books and newspapers he sold. The trains traveled to Detroit, Michigan. Al often read at the Detroit Public Library while waiting for his train home.

Learning about the Telegraph

When Al was 15 years old, he rescued a toddler who had wandered onto the train tracks. The baby's father was James MacKenzie, a telegraph operator.

In the 1860s, using a telegraph was the best way to communicate over long distances.

MacKenzie offered to teach Al how to work a telegraph as a thank-you for saving his child.

A telegraph could send messages over an electric wire. The messages traveled between telegraph stations. The telegraph used a system of dots and dashes called Morse code to relay messages.

Al enjoyed working with
the telegraph. By the age
of 16, he was working
as a telegraph operator
himself. He worked hard
to learn everything he
could about telegraphs.
In his free time, he
experimented with old
telegraph parts. He
thought about ways he
could make the telegraph
better.

Morse Code

Telegraphs use a system
called Morse code to spell
out messages. In Morse
code, a series of dots and
dashes represent letters
in the alphabet. Common
letters, such as e and i, are
represented by dots instead
of dashes since they are used
most often and are easier to
send. Whoever receives the
telegraph message translates
the dots and dashes into
letters and then into words to
form the message.

First Inventions

In 1868 Edison moved
to Boston, Massachusetts. He worked for Western
Union, a telegraph company. There, Edison created
an electric voting machine. With this invention, the
legislative voting process could be made faster.
Edison got a patent from the government for his

invention. But politicians were not interested in buying Edison's voting machine. They did not want to speed up their voting processes. Edison did not let that get in the way of his other inventions. He focused on the telegraph.

Rules of Invention

When Edison patented the voting machine in 1868, he thought he had created a useful product. The machine made voting quicker than writing a vote down on paper. But as it turned out, politicians did not care to speed up the voting process. The experience taught Edison an important lesson. When he was inventing something, it was important to think about whether it was something people would actually want.

Improving the Telegraph

In 1870 Edison opened a manufacturing shop in Newark, New Jersey. There, Edison and other people worked on improving the telegraph. The next year, Edison met Mary Stillwell. Edison fell in love with her, and the two married on December 25, 1871. A year later, they had a daughter, Marion.

Western Union's General Operating Department in 1875

In 1874 Edison invented his quadruplex telegraph system for Western Union. This system allowed operators to send four telegraph messages over one wire at the same time. Telegraph companies liked this idea because using fewer wires was cheaper. With the money he earned from the sale of his invention, Edison was able to expand his laboratory in Newark. He could not wait to invent more products.

CHAPTER TWO

CAPTURING SOUND

In 1876 Edison opened up another laboratory. It would be a laboratory for inventing, building, and testing products. The building also had an office and a library. Edison set up his new laboratory in Menlo Park, New Jersey. Edison chose Menlo Park because it was close to New York, where he could go to experiment on Western Union wires. Also, railways to both New York and Philadelphia ran through

Edison's Menlo Park laboratory had an office, in which Edison often studied and researched.

Menlo Park. This made it easy to get supplies from those cities.

Edison's laboratory was nicknamed the "invention factory." With this laboratory, Edison became the first inventor to employ an entire research team to experiment and develop new inventions. He hired different specialists to work with him. Some were machinists, and some were scientists. Together they worked to improve current products. They also tried inventing new products.

Edison's employees were hard workers. But no one seemed to work as hard as Edison. He often worked for 16 hours straight. He skipped sleeping many nights. Instead, he took naps in his laboratory during the day.

Happiness at Invention Factory

The workers at Edison's laboratory worked long hours. But many of them remembered their time there fondly. Edison had a large pipe organ at the back wall of the laboratory. Sometimes when the workers were staying up all night working, Edison would play the pipe organ and lead the group in song.

A New Telephone

Edison's dedication to inventing would pay off in a big way. On March 10, 1876, Scottish inventor Alexander Graham Bell invented the first telephone. Bell had worked out a way to change a person's voice into electric signals. Then he sent those signals to a receiver.

In Bell's telephone, sound waves from a person's voice caused a small metal disc, known as the transmitter diaphragm, to vibrate. This vibration created a current in the transmitter magnet, which then produced an electrical signal that could be transmitted over a wire to a receiver at the other end. The magnet in the receiver responded to the electrical signal and caused the receiver diaphragm to vibrate and reproduce the sound wave. Unfortunately, Bell's telephone could not be heard clearly when the signal was sent over a long wire.

Edison worked to create a better phone. In 1877 he finally had something. He discovered that inserting a piece of carbon between the diaphragm and the magnet improved the strength of the electrical signal. This carbon-button transmitter worked much better over longer distances and helped to make the telephone a success.

The Phonograph

That same year, Edison came up with a brand-new invention. His work with the new telephone gave him the idea. At first Edison wanted to find a way to record telephone messages. Then he started thinking about recording any sound. After many different designs, Edison created a device that could record and play back sounds. He called it the phonograph.

Edison's phonograph was made of a metal

Phonograph Doll

One of Edison's less successful inventions was a talking doll. The doll had a tiny phonograph inside its body. A child needed to turn the hand crank at a steady speed to play a prerecorded message. But these dolls were very expensive. They were also too delicate to play with.

Edison sits with his phonograph in 1878.

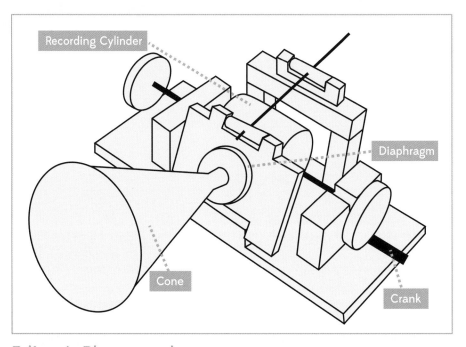

Edison's Phonograph
This diagram shows a smaller version of Edison's early phonograph. How does this image help you better understand how the phonograph works? Was it what you expected?

cylinder. The cylinder had a sheet of tinfoil wrapped around it. Edison turned a crank to rotate the cylinder. At the same time, he yelled into a cone that was attached to a diaphragm. The sound waves made the diaphragm vibrate. The vibrations pressed a metal pin, or stylus, into the tinfoil. The stylus made a dented pattern in the tinfoil based on the vibrations from Edison's voice. To play back the sound, Edison cranked the cylinder back. Then he put the stylus at its original place. The phonograph reproduced the sound as the stylus followed the track in the tinfoil.

The phonograph quickly became popular with the public. Edison thought that phonographs would be most successful in businesses. But people wanted the phonograph for a different reason—music. The phonograph made Edison famous. People started calling him the "wizard of Menlo Park." They could not wait to see what he would come up with next.

FURTHER EVIDENCE

There is a lot of information about Edison's first popular inventions in Chapter Two. But if you could pick out the main point of the chapter, what would it be? What evidence did the chapter provide to support this point? Visit the website below to learn more about Edison's inventions. Write a few sentences about the new information from the website as evidence to support the main point of this chapter.

Edison's Inventions
www.mycorelibrary.com/thomas-edison

CHAPTER THREE

LIGHTING UP THE WORLD

n fall 1878, Edison set a new goal. He wanted to create an incandescent, or glowing, electric light. At the time, there were already electric lights. They were called arc lights. They were used as streetlights and in lighthouses. But these lights were too bright to be used in homes. Instead people used candles or kerosene lamps to light their homes.

Thomas Edison is best known for his invention of the incandescent lightbulb.

Before the lightbulb, people used kerosene lamps for light.

An Incandescent Light

Edison wanted to make a light that was safe and affordable to use in a home. He was not the only one with this goal. Other inventors were already experimenting with incandescent lighting. An incandescent light is created by heating a material with an electric current until it produces a soft glow. But the heated material would often burn up or melt quickly, causing the light to go out.

Edison and other inventors had the basic idea of an incandescent light figured out. The light contained a base with two metal contacts. The contacts would be connected to an electric circuit. Each of the contacts was attached to contact wires. A filament ran between the contact wires. When connected to an electric source, a current would

Arc Lights

The first form of electric light was the arc light. British inventor Humphrey Davy first demonstrated the arc light in 1808 in England. Sending a spark between two carbon rods created the light. As the current passed from one rod to the other, it created a visible electric current through the air. This made an arc of light between the rods. However, the arc light had some downfalls. Hot sparks sometimes fell from the light and caused fires.

What Is an Electric Circuit?

An electric circuit happens when electricity travels through wires. In Edison's lightbulb, the contact wires formed a circuit between the power source and the filament. If one of the wires or the filament broke, the circuit was broken and the light would not appear.

run up the contact wires to the filament. The current would stimulate electrons, causing them to move around rapidly in the filament material. This movement gave off energy, heating up the filament. As the filament heated, it began to glow and give off light.

But oxygen in the air would cause the filament to burn up immediately. A burning filament could even cause a fire. A glass vacuum bulb closed up the contact wires and filament. This way oxygen could not get in.

Finding a Filament

But even in a glass vacuum, the filament would not last long. Edison's main challenge was finding a material for the filament that would not burn up

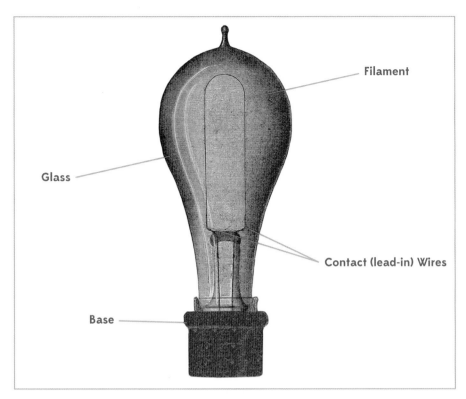

Edison's Lightbulb
This diagram shows the parts of the incandescent lightbulb Edison invented. After reading about Edison's creation of the lightbulb, what did you imagine the inside of it would look like? How does seeing the parts of the lightbulb help you better understand how it works?

quickly. He even tried fishing line and human hair. Finally, he found that carbonized thread would glow for at least 40 hours. To carbonize thread, Edison had to bake the thread in an oven until it was charred.

People were excited about Edison's incandescent light, or lightbulb. As word spread, more and more

Edison and his workers tested many different materials to find a filament for his lightbulb.

people wanted these electric lights in their homes. Edison had created the product for which he would be most famous. But he had more inventions up his sleeve.

It took Edison many tries to perfect the lightbulb. Some people were annoyed with how long it took Edison to create a lightbulb that could be used outside the laboratory. In 1880 one critic wrote about Edison's slow progress:

> *What a happy man Mr. Edison must be! Three times within the short space of 18 months he has had the glory of finally and triumphantly solving a problem of world-wide interest. . . . If he continues to observe the same strict economy of practical results which has hitherto characterized his efforts in electric lighting, there is no reason why he should not for the next 20 years completely solve the problem of electric light twice a year without in any way interfering with its interest or novelty.*
>
> Source: "The Great Edison Scare." Journal of Gas Lighting. January 20, 1880. Print.

Viewpoints

What seems to be the opinion or viewpoint of the author who wrote the above passage about Edison's lightbulb? How does it differ from the viewpoints expressed in Chapter Three? Write a short essay comparing the two points of view.

CHAPTER FOUR

A NEW LABORATORY

Edison's lightbulb made him more popular than ever. But he knew that for the lightbulb to be successful, people needed access to electricity in their homes. He helped create the first commercial power station in New York City in September 1882. The station provided electricity to homes within one square mile (3 sq km). This allowed people to use Edison's electric lights in their homes

Edison works in his new laboratory in West Orange, New Jersey.

The Electric Age

With the first commercial power station, Edison started a time period called the electric age. Before this time, homes did not have access to electricity. People had to use the light of candles or kerosene lamps to see in the dark. These lights were not ideal because they flickered. They also posed a fire risk. As more houses were connected to electricity through power stations, Edison and other inventors could bring electric lights and appliances into people's homes.

and businesses. Before long, more power stations popped up around the country. Electricity was becoming more accessible.

Life Changes

Although Edison's career was going well, he soon suffered a personal tragedy when his wife, Mary, died unexpectedly in 1884. In February 1886, Edison remarried. His new wife was Mina Miller. Mina was the daughter of an inventor and manufacturer, and she took a personal interest in Edison's work. In 1887 Edison built a new laboratory in West Orange, New Jersey. It was known as the Laboratory of Thomas A. Edison or the Edison

Laboratory. Edison and his staff continued to dream up new products.

The Motion Picture Camera

After learning how to capture sound with the phonograph, Edison had a new goal. He wanted to create a device that captured moving pictures. With the help of experimenter and photographer William Dickson and machinist Charles Brown, Edison created a motion picture camera in 1892. He also made the kinetoscope, which was used to view the film.

Edison's motion picture camera used a long strip of flexible film wound onto a wheel. Then the camera would take many pictures very quickly of something in motion. When all these pictures were viewed quickly through the kinetoscope, the picture would appear to be moving as each image showed a slightly different scene. To use the kinetoscope, the viewer had to look through a small peephole.

Unlike movies today, only one person could view the kinetoscope at a time.

A Failure

While Edison's motion picture camera was a huge success, some of his other inventions were not. In fact he failed more often than he succeeded when experimenting. In the 1890s Edison suffered a large failure. The demand for steel was increasing in the United States. It was needed for construction. Steel is made mainly of iron. Edison wanted to develop a machine that could process leftover iron from mines where iron had already been removed. This iron was embedded in rock. Edison hoped to use a magnet powered by electricity to remove iron from crushed rock.

Edison invested millions of dollars into this idea. But the machinery used to process the iron kept breaking down. Finally the price of iron decreased. This meant it was unlikely that much money would be made off its sale. Edison abandoned the project. But his failure did little to affect his work. Edison spent even more time in his lab, working on sound-recording technology and electric storage batteries, among other projects.

EXPLORE ONLINE

Chapter Four mentions Edison's new laboratory in West Orange, New Jersey. The website below offers more information about the laboratory. What are the similarities between Chapter Four and the information you found on the website? Are there any differences? How do the two sources present information differently?

The Invention Factory
www.mycorelibrary.com/thomas-edison

CHAPTER FIVE

LEAVING A LEGACY

**A**s Edison grew older, he spent more time promoting his products than inventing new ones. Being one of the most famous people in the world also kept him busy. People invited him to events and held award ceremonies in his honor. At age 60, Edison declared that he would no longer pursue commercial inventions. After all of his tinkering with new inventions, Edison just wanted

As he aged, Edison only wanted to work in his laboratory as a scientist, not an inventor.

Other Inventions

Edison's phonograph, lightbulb, and motion picture camera are his most famous inventions. But Edison and his team created more than 1,000 patents during his lifetime. Some of these inventions include a fruit preserver, an electric pen, a battery-powered fan, and houses and furniture made out of concrete.

to explore. Edison's laboratory in West Orange continued to run. The laboratory worked more on improving Edison's existing inventions than creating new ones. At age 64, Edison left most of the operations of the laboratory to others.

A New Position

In 1915 the US government asked Edison to head the Naval Consulting Board. There was conflict in Europe. The United States was gearing up for what would be World War I (1914–1918). The Naval Consulting Board was a group of talented US scientists and inventors that could help the Armed Forces by providing new technology. During the war, 70-year-old Edison worked on inventions that could detect

Famous automobile inventor Henry Ford, left, and Edison were great friends.

submarines. Although the board did not contribute much to the war, it would serve as a model for similar collaborations in the future.

Always an Inventor

As he aged, Edison suffered from diabetes and stomach problems. Although he slowed down, he

Honors for a Legend

Edison received many awards and mentions for his work. In 1928 the US Congress awarded him a Medal of Honor for a lifetime of achievement. A year later, a grand party was held to celebrate the incandescent light. Edison was honored with a banquet and recognized again for this invention.

never truly stopped inventing. In the late 1920s, Edison's good friend and automobile inventor Henry Ford asked Edison for help. Ford wanted Edison to find a material that could be used for car wheels. Usually rubber from the milky sap of rubber trees was used. Edison tried to find another plant that could grow well in the United States and be used to make rubber.

Edison tested thousands of different plants that he thought could be used for tire material. He concluded that goldenrod, a weed with yellow flowers, showed the most promise. But at

Edison sits with his wife, Mina, during an interview on his eighty-fourth birthday on February 11, 1931.

80 years old, he became too sick to continue these experiments.

Good-Bye to a Great Inventor

In August 1931, Edison collapsed at his home. From there, his health got worse. Edison died on October 18, 1931. The president at the time,

Herbert Hoover, called for a moment of silence and darkness to honor him. On October 22, at 10:00 p.m., Americans turned off their electric lights in remembrance of the inventor.

Edison is still remembered today through his inventions—some that we still use every day. But he is also celebrated for teaching the world about the science of invention and the importance of curiosity.

Electric Cars

Electric cars may seem like a new phenomenon, but Edison tried out this idea beginning in 1899. At the time, cars were still a new invention. Edison wanted to create a battery for cars. It would be used as fuel instead of gasoline. He wanted the battery to last for 100 miles (161 km) before needing to recharge. But by the time Edison and his team perfected the new battery in 1908, gasoline had already become the favored fuel for cars.

A 1931 article in the *New York Times* announced Edison's death:

> *Thomas Alva Edison died at 3:24 o'clock this morning at his home. . . . The great inventor, the fruits of whose genius so magically transformed the everyday world, was 84 years and 8 months old. . . . Through the long days . . . he calmly, cheerfully awaited the inevitable. . . . Anxiety for the man whose creative genius gave the world the electric light, the phonograph, the motion picture camera and a thousand of other inventions ranging through all the various fields of science had been general since he collapsed in the living room of his home on Aug. 1.*

Source: "Thomas Edison Dies in Coma at 84; Family With Him as the End Comes." New York Times. October 18, 1931. Print.

Consider Your Audience

Read this passage closely. Think about how you would change it for a different audience, such as Edison's fellow scientists, his family, or someone who has never heard of Edison. Write a new article conveying the same information directed at a new audience. How is your approach different from the original text and why?

The Film Industry

Thomas Edison's motion picture camera made it possible to film movies. Although Edison's kinetoscope allowed only one person to view a movie at a time, it was the start of movies as entertainment.

The Lightbulb

Edison's basic lightbulb design is still used today. Before lightbulbs, people had to use the light of candles or kerosene lamps to see in the dark. These lights were not ideal because they flickered. They also posed a fire risk. Edison's lightbulb made it more possible for people to stay up late into the evenings, working or having fun. Updated streetlights made transportation at night safer too.

The Music Industry

Edison's phonograph brought a way for music to be recorded and played back. Many see this as the start of the modern music industry. Music became something that people could record and listen to again and again. For some time, Edison even had his own recording business.

The Process of Innovation

Edison invented products and technology we still use today. But his most influential invention was his process of innovation. Edison was the first inventor to head a research laboratory. He employed a whole team of researchers for the creation of new inventions.

STOP AND THINK

Say What?

Learning about Edison's inventions can mean learning a lot of new vocabulary. Find five words in this book that you have never seen or heard before. Use a dictionary to find out what they mean. Then write the meanings in your own words. Use each word in a new sentence.

Surprise Me

Chapter Three discusses Edison's invention of the lightbulb. You probably turn on a lightbulb at least once every day. What two or three facts about the lightbulb did you find the most surprising? Write a few sentences about each fact. Why did they surprise you?

Why Do I Care?

Edison lived and worked nearly 100 years ago. But he had a major impact on your life through his inventions. How do Edison's inventions affect your life today? How would your life be different if Edison had never lived?

You Are There

This book discusses what it was like to work on inventions. Imagine that you are a worker in Edison's laboratory. You are working on the invention of the lightbulb. What are your days like? How do you feel about your work? What is it like working for Edison?

GLOSSARY

incandescent
giving off light as a result of being heated

kerosene
a flammable oil

laboratory
a room or building used for science experiments

machinist
a person who operates, builds, or makes repairs to machines

operator
a person who runs a machine

patent
a government document that gives someone the rights to own and sell a new invention

transmitter
something that sends signals from one place to another

vacuum
a container from which all air has been removed

vibration
a series of small, fast movements

LEARN MORE

Books

Adkins, Jan. *Thomas Edison*. New York: DK Publishing, 2009.

Barretta, Gene. *Timeless Thomas: How Thomas Edison Changed Our Lives*. New York: Henry Holt, 2012.

Garcia, Tracy J. *Thomas Edison*. New York: PowerKids Press, 2013.

Websites

To learn more about Great Minds of Science, visit **booklinks.abdopublishing.com**. These links are routinely monitored and updated to provide the most current information available.

Visit **www.mycorelibrary.com** for free additional tools for teachers and students.

INDEX

ABOUT THE AUTHOR

Katherine Krieg is the author of many books for young people. When she was in the fifth grade, she was in a play about Thomas Edison. She played the part of a worker in Edison's factory.